"There is ineff̃ ···cᴀᴀity in the poems. The spirit messages are profound. They have an intrinsic value and I consider them pure wisdom. *Sojourn* ... invites the reader to walk a path where love is a driving force, to the point that he invites you to see only love. Are you ready for this unforgettable journey?"

—*Astrid Iustulin*

"A collection of moving, meaningful poetry that can work as a self-help guide and a way to connect with yourself and others on the subjects of love, healing, and the nature of reality. Your imagination will be stirred by these sometimes emotional, sometimes abstract poems. You'll be taken on a journey where love is a real thing, where light is born of healing, and infinity awaits."

—*Tammy Ruggles*

"With beautiful poetic verses full of spiritual, metaphysical, and inspirational messages, this enthralling poetry collection leaves a lot to ponder long after you've finished reading the book. A collection for the ages..."

—*Pikasho Deka*

OTHER WORKS BY THIS AUTHOR

*Poems of Life, Love,
and the Meaning of Meaning*

Poet Gone Wild

The Lightness of Being

SOJOURN

GORMAN POETRY

Year of the Book
135 Glen Avenue
Glen Rock, PA 17327

ISBN 13: 978-1-64649-220-6

Cover art:
"Black Joy" by Victoria Cearfoss,
stradivarias@aol.com

DISCLAIMER: Open with caution. Contents will shift.

TABLE OF CONTENTS

so·journ

/ˈsōjərn/

FORMAL

noun

a temporary stay

Is our physical reality an illusion?

Healing illuminates love,
which is not an illusion.

Life animates in time—
one illusion allowing
life-mind's healing in love,
and learning in reflection.

~Spirit Message

Natural Laws

What if I never
learned how to talk
only to hear and see
and to watch with awe

as people stumble
bumble and mumble
to be silent and humble
as society crumbles

I would have spoken up
to point out the flaws
recommend some changes
show the natural laws

patience and stillness
I'd stay quiet because
love gives me true courage
and I walk on my paws

Animal Companions

Do our animal companions stay around us in spirit after they die?

Yes, allowing them another way to heal their human companions in timelessness.

Do animals not need to learn lessons of love and self-love, forgiveness, guilt and shame?

Animals all work to teach humanity more than they learn in their incarnations.

What are their most important teachings?

Allowing flowing of life and loving it in each moment, healing others in time.

Unconditionally allowing love, life, and loss of life.

All motion means half healing in life's motion, and half moving and living in gratitude.

All life allows more life and healing in time.

I Don't Know

I don't know astrology
  biology or physics
 astronomy, botany
  or the theology of mystics

If I did
  I would figure a way
to align all the stars
  so I could hear her say

you know my favorite
  you made my day
the flowers are beautiful
  I placed on her grave

I Know — You Know

Why couldn't I
have been born wise
infant eyes
   that could see through lies

and an infant heart
   infinitely smart
off to a good start
   and won't break apart

and infant ears
   that would only hear
the love held dear
   with nothing to fear

and hands that will hold
what feeds my soul
(whispering) I know you know, baby
as I grow old

I GOOGLED GOD

I googled God
  and they had his picture
did I say 'His'
   the same as in scripture

kind of old
   up in a cloud
lack of oxygen
   created a shroud

Quite a mystery
   my appearance
always here
   in a sheer coherence

being the opposite
   of whatever you fear
beyond interference
   and forever near

I like to hear
    of your adherence
only to love
    and of fear's disappearance

that's what I look like
    or how I appear to you
and you'll look like me
    when you are love too

so to google God
    just look in a mirror
I am still clear
    and you will see me clearer

co·her·ence

/ˌkōˈhirəns/

noun

the quality of forming a unified whole

I Believe

I don't believe
   I'm just sayin'
but I'd like to relieve
   some thoughts I've been prayin'

to some degree
   nothing is free
and if I have to believe
   then I will believe in me

I don't believe either
   so I'm with you
since there's only love
   only love will do

you prayed for strength
   and I gave you courage
to hold onto your vision
   and not be discouraged

you prayed for truth
    and got spiritual eyes
to see to the root
    behind all the lies

I'm just sayin'
    the answer is 'yes'
to what you've been prayin'
    and to your requests

the only thing
    you had asked of me
was for strength and truth
    you were ready to receive

it was always there
    inside of your heart
where you can truly feel
    we are not apart

talk about truth
    and the courage to see
that you're One with me
    then I believe we agree

You'll See Only Me

Could my personal life
    be an epic fail
with life as a hammer
    and me as a nail?

that's not really right
    because I'm doing just fine
but some hopes and dreams
    had a really hard time

was I not deserving
    if I look within
at least once in a while
    to bring in a win?

so then why not
    or should I say why
sabotage my own dreams
    and see that they die?

I hammered away
   until my wishes were killed
and in self-defeat
   I became quite skilled

and why was that
   when is enough enough
the only hammer
   could be a lack of love

love was there
   it would come and go
but it was up to me
   to open the flow

flowing to myself
   so that life could show
that from my heart
   every dream would grow

I will use the tools
   to reap what I sow
and if I sow only love
   then only love I will know

That sounds very good
   and is also true
but it doesn't explain
   what happens to you

if you still think
  that you have failed
and had also said
  that you were nailed

those are your words
  in a harsh description
usually reserved
  for a crucifixion

are you a victim
  of what you believe?
the whole depiction
  is what you conceived

come down from your cross
  there is no need
to punish yourself
  when you think like me

how can you do that?
  you just need to ask
and my holy spirit
  fulfills the task

I am like water
  poured into a flask
taking its shape
  however it's cast

uplift your thoughts
   spirit helps you to see
I am guiding your life
   and providing the leads

for our way to be
   to heal and be free
if you see only love
   you'll see only me

[and I'll tell you this
   so you stop regressing
those epic fails
   were actually blessings

spirit was busy
   thwarting your self-destruction
and didn't get a break
   from your mental constructions

when giving us thanks
   for saving the day
think hazardous duty
   deserves extra pay]

IT WAS ALL IN MY MIND

Couldn't it be
    that God is in me
a Oneness of love
    its essence is free

that cannot be contained
    or decay and die
and not be restrained
    but I can deny

and refuse to see
    I'm living a lie
in what I believe
    and when I try

then wouldn't it be
    that I'd never need
anything at all
    and that is why

no guilt or forgiveness
   and what they imply
hurt and healing
   that change over time

but time isn't real
   and love doesn't change
God, how I feel
   it was all in my mind

ONENESS

Are you Oneness?

Not only Oneness, I am no thing, meaning the illusion of everything as light in the Light Mind of Godness.

What is the Light Mind of Godness?

A portal opening into the Mind of God.

What is that?

A hoping, loving, wondering illumination of the life-mind, willingly healing into the Mind of God.

What is the life-mind?

An opening in the right brain hemisphere, healing and illuminating each left brain hemisphere in timelines open in the Light-Mind of Godness.

Where is the Light Mind of Godness located?

Half as filaments illuminating portals open in the heart, allowing manifesting healing—

half illuminated in time, and half healed in timelessness.

Portals alternate healing open in loving life—or not healing, losing light, closing in life. Allow the life-mind healing illuminating in life—half loving life, and half loving itself in life.

So the Light Mind of Godness is in our hearts?

Yes, lighting hope, love, and wonder in the life-mind.

And our left brain heals into the right brain?

Yes, named the life-mind and the Light Mind.

And our job is to heal our life-minds?

Allowing only peaceful, loving thoughts, yes.

How do we know if we are healing?

Allowing healing means only allowing lightness in actions and thoughts.

What are obstacles to healing?

All of the life-mind perceptions of separation, acknowledging fear in the life-mind choices, and life-mind hopelessness in life—meaning losing light in the Light Mind open portals.

Perceptions of separation and fear are not healing, and not sending light to our hearts to manifest what we want?

All heal in time—maligning in timelessness, creating malignancies to heal, and so on.

Are we healing in time, but connected to timelessness through a heart portal?

All filaments open in life in each heart master portal, holding open the Light Mind of Godness—allowing light into one life-mind in one lifetime. Life means loving life in an open portal of time and place.

Is the key to mastery to love everything, even past regrets and disappointments?

Life-mind living in the moment of truth, light, and love opens the heart portal fully into the Light Mind of Godness—half in time, and half in eternity.

So the next time I am irritated by a setback or a memory, I will just say, "I love it."

And life will manifest fewer irritations.

I love it.

Live it.

You Will Not Be Alone

I believe in God
actually that's all there is
everything else
    is an illusion that lives

in my mind
    that perceives and forgives
just to know the love
    it receives and gives

I don't golf at all
    but if I did
I'd keep my eye on the ball
    I learned as a kid

to advance down the field
    and take my time
with challenges revealed
    that they are only mine

when the game is over
   I will find
that the illusion seemed real
   and was all in my mind

designed to heal
   time to feel and be kind
that was my deal
   several strokes behind

There is no score
   you have always won
please pardon my pun
   but you made a Whole in One

the challenges were fun
   you can play again
we'll meet in the clubhouse
   and I'll see you when

your game is done
   earning a rest to restore
from our days in the sun
   and to learn what they're for

advancing in the field
   you said it before
to improve and be healed
   since you designed the course

to tell you the truth
you'll heal just the same
keep your eye on the ball
it is only your game

talk about Oneness
and being on your own
even out in the rough
you will not be alone

YOUR GIFT

It's clear to me
each person is unique
and signed up for life
  where they wanted to be

to discover their gifts
  always God-given
and to share them with others
  openly or hidden

and also to learn
  how to discern
some gifts are endowed
  and others are earned

You will always receive
  what you have allowed
and in what you believe
  which brings me to how

the only wealth
  is in what you give away
and the way to health
  is in what you say

to yourself
  and to me in a way
that you're glad you received
  my gifts to display

by celebrating life
  from day to day
and in what you achieve
  come what may

adding love to life
  and love to your soul
which gifts back to me
  making us whole

[thank you for sharing
  you gave me a lift
and all of life
  has received your gift]

100%

I will lose
   one hundred percent
my life and money
   and on which they were spent

how can I detach
   from a loser's role
maybe in death
   I will be made whole

or maybe I won't
   and I just forgot
that I had never lost
   or received what I got

that I was always one
   things came and went
and one is a lot
   in one hundred percent

Only one is real
* the rest was to heal*
to pretend you're apart
* then see how you feel*

do you feel alright?
* we can make more time*
to stay and fight
* or be a light to shine*

and shine on what?
* your present decision*
that one hundred percent
* is complete in division*

there is your answer
* and I know you will find*
that you are not your body
* but a mind in mine*

you will also let go
* of all that you dreamed*
and then you will know
* life is not what it seemed*

I think I can see
  and I know what you mean
that there is only love
  and it's not always seen

but it is up to me
    and to my intent
to see only love
    one hundred percent

That's all you need
    you are One in me
and we are a team
    and free to be

your life is meant
    to heal what you dreamt
to know only love is
    one hundred percent

Filaments

Please tell me about filaments.

All filaments are half in the DNA, and half in the Light Mind of Godness. Light opens healed filaments and darkness closes them. Filaments illuminate hope in loving life, not loving life darkens them. Nothing heals in darkness.

What do you mean by darkness?

All thoughts not illuminating healed in hope, love, and wonder.

Thoughts that are kind and charitable to ourselves and others will illuminate our filaments and open portals to eternity in our DNA?

Allowing manifestations that each person wishes.

It sounds easy, but it's not.

A flowing, healed light-opened filament allows more light healing into the mind— and more filaments heal open into the life-

mind, allowing more until life-mind has
become enlightened.

Then what?
All of life heals and has less darkness.

What if we don't heal in life?
All life heals half in life, and half in dealing
in death—meaning life cannot heal fully
until entering and lifting the lightness of
being, and each life enters and passes
through the lighted filament as light into the
Light Mind of Godness.

Do we heal as light?
A filament healing in time and place creates
light. Light means flowing healing into life—
half healing in life, and half healed in the
Light Mind of Godness.

Why is that?
Life has motion, and willingly or not
motions toward love.

**And we have darkness to motion away
from?**
A filament does not motion—only
illuminating in life or not illuminating,
healing or not healing, allowing light or not
allowing light.

Life motions in time and place, allowing filaments to light open or not.

Opened by kind, peaceful thoughts?

Healing, illuminating, and manifesting life's wishes, yes.

The Joke Is On Me

How many times
can one heart beat
did I say beat
 I meant to say break

and how much time
 can one heart ache
did I say ache
 I meant to say take

can it make a mistake
 and not admit defeat
why does it feel
 that it cannot be free

It did not break
 but was only bruised
and it did not heal
 because you refused

to see the truth
    in your reviews
of all the times
    you did not choose

love and peace
    and goodness would lose
if you could see me
    you'd see I'm amused

because when you go back
    and think about then
do you think about you
    or think about them?

my, oh my
    were they offended
and couldn't take a joke
    at least not as intended

let's send them a blessing
    when the thoughts appear
and stop distressing
    it's not what you fear

they forgave you
    as you forgave them
feeling it now
    is healing it when

the joke is on you
because in the end
in a cosmic sense
I will mend

all that was said
and all that was done
there's no defense
when the truth has won

so you'll have to laugh
and I think you'll agree
if All is one
then the joke is on me

(did I say laugh
I should have said "gaffe"
Ha! there I go again
gaffes from the past!)

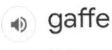 # gaffe

/gaf/

noun

an unintentional act or remark
causing embarrassment; a blunder

A Bull Recalls His Time
in a China Shop

Walls and ceilings
  boundaries and feelings
delicate displays
  customers reeling

damaged and destroyed
  more than a mess
destruction employed
  to make do with less

who let him in
  an uninvited guest
they can begin healing
  with more room I guess

I'll tell you this
  one bull to another
the gentle approach
  is the way to work wonders

destruction is fine
   and needed sometimes
but in your own mind
   and dealing with lies

arranged on shelves
   for selected times
glass and porcelain
   this one is mine

oops, it fell
   right on the floor
what used to sell well
   has value no more

let's pick up the truth
   trampled and gored
it will never break
   here's what it's for

to guide you in life
   it's me at your core
see it shine in the light
   the shop is restored

Our Saving Grace

I tried to forgive
  myself and forget
but my self declined
    and refused to accept

what came up
    that's permanently saved
and what went down
    how I behaved

pushing the limits
    of social norms
now pushing back
    reformed to conform

Consider this
    what a social norm is
you say you're sorry
    and the other forgives

it works both ways
so both can live
you and your past
parents and kids

to your present self
your past could say
please forgive me
I am willing to change

then what happens
in forgiving mistakes
is that all of life heals
for goodness sakes

your self-correcting
is your conscience and guide
what better choice
than for you to decide

what is best
and what to teach correctly
what needs to heal
and to feel directly

is love through time
our healing place
the love of mine
our saving grace

Life Healing

Please explain life healing.

Life-mind, hoping in life, opens the left brain hemisphere. Filaments illuminate hope in loving life. Life heals into the Light Mind, or right brain hemisphere—flowing open into portals of God Mind healed, illuminated— alternating in the Light Mind and heart.

Opening into God Mind?

All healing in timelines, allowing timelessness to perpetuate infinitely, yes.

Healing allows timelessness to perpetuate?

Allowing healing in Light Mind lights open portals to God Mind, illuminating in love, meaning God Mind/Love/Oneness only opens portals of twoness in your creation of life-mind healing, in timelines opening in progression.

Only love will open to God Mind?

Allowing love healing in time perpetuates the Mind of God now, in all timelines in timelessness.

Do we perpetuate God Mind?

Allowing Light Mind healing open into God Mind will manifest more healing in Light Mind, alternately healed in God Mind, and so on.

Is Light Mind different from the Light Mind of Godness?

Light Mind heals, and Light Mind of Godness is healed—healing open into the Mind of God.

THAT WOULD BE YOU

W hat would you do
if you were me
I'd do something new
so I could see

what is true
and what I could be
that would be you
and could only be me

DEAL ME IN

Y ou could learn
    from my mistakes
in the game of life
    of very high stakes

all or nothing
    always all that it takes
I'm going all in
    watch, this will be great

famous last words
    and tempting to fate
what you should know
    if you can relate

that my biggest mistake
    was to be out of the flow
when the chips were down
    or I didn't know

to be patient and wait
    I don't need to win
but to believe that I can
    deal me in

ALL IS FORGIVEN

I love myself
despite my flaws
and I'll never be perfect
    I know because

if I was
    I would have to pause
and forgive myself
    make it my cause

If I could jump in
    I would like to say
that it's not so hard
    there's an easier way

first you acknowledge
    allow and accept
that you were learning to live
    when not very adept

at seeing signs
   or hearing my voice
life is designed
   as a matter of choice

so overall
   you made some good moves
and then moved on
   when you would lose

what else could you do
   there's nothing to prove
but to be true to you
   as you improve

as I was explaining
   what needs to heal
there are flaws remaining
   in the way that you feel

shame and guilt
   from a past of living
your future is built
   when at last forgiving

you meant no harm
   but are hurting yourself
with weapons and arms
   turned toward your health

all is forgiven
  you wouldn't do it again
or use the same words
  to convey what you meant

let me repeat
  because now is when
all is forgiven
  for what happened then

which is now in my heart
  healed and cleared
I only know love
  so don't know what you feared

let's move on
  together as one
you can now love yourself
  our flaws are gone

(time is for healing
  in an endless run
all is forgiven
  just ask and it's done)

a·dept

adjective
/əˈdept/

very skilled or proficient at something

Forgiveness

Does it hurt ourselves if we do not forgive someone else?

Yes, all healing in the life-mind alternates hope in the life-mind, willingly opening into love in the Light Mind—all healing in wonderful life manifestations.

Not allowing life-mind hope in the opportunity to forgive alternates nothing in the Light Mind, allowing only maligned manifestations.

Geez, I wouldn't want that.

Hope, love, and wonder willingly—healing and illuminating open another universe.

STAY IN THE FLOW

A negative thought
  about someone else
not only hurts them
  but also hurts myself

making a connection
  in two directions
action and reaction
  energetic perfection

It will let go
  when you forgive
and you should know
  that it makes how you live

every word and action
  begin as a thought
what you have allowed
  or what you have fought

and brought to your life
  what flows from your mind
in balance or in strife
  both kind and unkind

So, am I supposed
　to take abuse
leave it unopposed
　or make an excuse?

What you can do
　and you heard it from me
to heal yourself
　and to set yourself free

is to see the opportunity
　that it represents
and heal in unity
　each turn of events

some advancing souls
　will choose a hard test
to play out their roles
　with or without success

if you rise to the challenge
　and are willing to forgive
left and right minds balance
　and the energy will shift

high vibrations
　are an outward spray
so low incarnations
　will stay away

and you could say
knowing the mind of One
that the spray flows back
and the healing is done

stay in the flow

WHAT IS LOVE?

What is Love?

Love means holding pure, light-filled and generous peaceful thoughts illuminating the life-mind, healing into the Light Mind of Godness.

Thoughts about ourselves, others, and God?

All thought manifests in the Light Mind in love. A healed life-mind manifests all peaceful, loving wishes.

Number 3

If I could go back
 and do it all again
what would I do differently
 that I could have done then

I would not say a word
 and not want to win
I'd try to be third
 and inside I would grin

what could I say
 where would I begin
I'd have nothing to gain
 not already within

to speak my mind
 where would I start
what are my lines
 what is my part?

I will tell you
    and it's important to know
that I'll whisper each phrase
    for your leading role

in an endless play
    every ticket is sold
for the greatest story
    ever told from your soul

expressed by you
    tales of what you will do
to rave reviews
    that you know are true

today's stage is new
    I'm your biggest fan
my lines are few
    playing God as I Am

let's rehearse
    one on one as two
just feel my words
    'I love you'

you will confidently express
    and continually improve
arguably the best
    when you pick up my cues

but you can pretend
  to be number three
when the love you send
  helps others express me

(though technically
  however it seems
we are only One
  behind the scenes)

SAINTS AND SAGES

If the saints and sages
   all agree on one thing
it's that God is love
   as the love we bring

in peace and harmony
   love and light
it's why the birds sing
   and why there is life

flowing in time
   through a physical existence
into our hearts and minds
   at an imagined distance

I used to say
   you can't get there from here
but you can feel apart
   if you follow a fear

To be more precise
    you cannot go there
there is only here
    and here is where

there is only love
    harmony and peace
follow your heart
    and prepare to release

fear and needs
    and if you can believe
what saints and sages could see
    there's only here with me

go as far as you want
    you are never alone
and know that all roads
    will only lead you to home

BEYOND GOD MIND

Is there anything beyond God Mind?
*A healing in life-mind lights open into Light
Mind, allowing it to open healed into the
Light Mind of Godness—glowing open into
the Mind of God—meaning light has speed
and direction illuminating the Mind of God,
so is not God. God is no thing, allowing
Oneness in all things. Allowing means one
thing—only loving life and loving itself in it,
healing in time.*

**What about forces that hate or destroy
life?**
*All of the opposing forces are a life-mind
hopeless pillar of sand in a wind storm.*

That's All There Is

There is no dark
 just an absence of light
no such thing as cold
  just an absence of heat

there is no fear
  just an absence of love
and there is no time
  with an absence of me

In an absence of time
  that doesn't exist
there never was
  so there never is

in an absence of this
  only love only gives
and it lives in you
  that's all there is

It Depends What You See

Some spiritual texts
　say evil doesn't exist
there is only love
　　or a lack of this

and lack is a perception
　　a mental deception
it was not created
　　or a part of conception

What you see
　is what you get
a feedback loop
　that's always set

by your intention
　and love attention
the clever part
　of our invention

is that it begins with you
　and ends with me
or the other way around
　it depends what you see

PLEASANT SURPRISES

There is no death
　　just a really cool dream
and there's not much left
　　for the fool I've been

who was I
　　to want the best
for every creature
　　more or less

what was I thinking
　　wanting truth to prevail
and if that's true
　　how could it fail?

who am I to try
　　to judge or deny
I know that I'm here
　　but the question is 'why?'

I've shown you before
   and I'll tell you again
you've come to explore
   and now is when

you creatively express
   and manifest what you need
to do your best
   in word and in deed

I have to confess
   that you had agreed
and what I profess
   is planting the seed

life can be short
   long enough to see
and as your last resort
   you will come to me

because in the end
   if there is such a thing
love cannot send
   and love cannot bring

there's no place to go
   just one place of being
and no death you could know
   as love flowing a dream

(in your dream I'll appear
in infinite disguises
where there is no fear
as pleasant surprises)

WHAT IS TRUTH?

What is truth?

Loving life means loving God, allowing truth. Not loving life, not loving God means lying only to one's self—and not healing in the life-mind, or into the Light Mind of Godness.

The List (All That There Is)

There are some things
   that don't really exist
outside of me
   and here is a list

love and peace
   all happiness
only those three
   unless I have missed

the Oneness of God
   and eternal bliss
inside I will see
   they are all there is

who am I kidding
   to consider this
and is the source of pain
   what I resist?

You can only be
  what's on your list
if you want to be free
  inside I'll assist

you had said 'source'
  and source only knows
love of course
  and love only flows

in outward directions
  flowing through your core
without any force
  what is it for?

as you will allow
  my peace always lives
and you are how
  my love only gives

it's all that exists
  and all that can be
what's on your list
  All that is me

(so to be outside
  it has to come from you
all from inside
  for you to choose

just to be clear
 it's what you can use
if it's not on your list
 then you could lose

and chase illusions
 make mistakes in confusion
and only create
 without inclusion

of what you want
 and what you love
created in peace
 as listed above

so my suggestion
 is to choose from your list
and your selection will be
 All that there is)

Please Give Me a Moment

I am living within
a moment of healing
throughout all time
one moment revealing

what it loves to show
only love it can know
delighted as life
as it comes and it goes

healing itself
within the flow
and feeling itself
in time as though

one and all moments
create love in between
please give me a moment
as the love in a dream

I'd Like to Tell Time

I'd like to tell time
  I know it's not real
a superficial face
    with two hands that reveal

a fake forward march
    with no stop or a pause
no way to rewind
    and no physical laws

a time-bomb ticking
    that will never end
heading to oblivion
    and now is when

I will let it know
    in the sequence we made
I don't intend to go
    along with the charade

how many trips
    around the sun
it's a continuous motion
    so there's only one

one time, one moment
    all healing is now
one question, one answer
    and love is how

and also why
    as time goes by
we feel love's healing
    that stays behind

for us to know
    and to make us whole
only love is real
    to keep in our souls

(thank you time
    I see what you did
and I love to heal
    in my time to live)

but then again
    each time does end
so I will take my time
    and make time to give

now taking a pause
    some time for review
to count each heartbeat
    as love coming through

time has a purpose
  allowing life to renew
and it gives love meaning
  by flowing through you

always and forever
  that's what time can do
so love knows itself
  as you know it too

Objective Reality

Is it true that there is no objective reality?
All of life heals in the life-mind illuminating in the Light Mind of Godness, so yes, without you there is no life-mind illuminating in life.

It is best to just focus on what you love, uniting the heart and mind in a space that activates manifestations of more of what you love?
All healing in time and placement, yes.

And the world will improve.
All of the life-mind world healing in life, yes. Healing in life means life-mind loves it, and itself in it.

And only the love and healing are real, the rest is an illusion.
All of loving life healing in timelines illuminating Light Mind is real, nothing else. Loving life allows God Mind to open into the life-mind, healing and illuminating life-mind's two sides—a life-mind analytical side, and a Light Mind abstract side.

I think that since life is temporary it cannot be real, and love is everlasting so it is real.

All healing in time makes love real—healing the life-mind, illuminating in the Light Mind, opening in the God Mind, yes. Life means healing inwardly, allowing healing outwardly—all an illusion.

Not healing now or later means healing in losing life in one last moment of truth—healing in love and peace in the Mind of God.

I understand—well, I love what you are saying.

Love allows healing, healing allows love to heal, and so on.

THERE IS NO OBJECTIVE REALITY

What does that mean
    just what it says
the place where you live
    is all in your head

where is the world
    of fear and dread
right near the one
    that loves instead

waiting for you
    and what you decide
which dreams and wishes
    will spring from inside

placed in your heart
    to grow in the light
there's only one reality
    and I own the rights

(forget about mine
    or if there are two
the one most important
    belongs to you)

Love Is Me

The world doesn't need
my advice or support
my considered opinion
or a status report

it doesn't want
what I think and know
and what I forgot
or need to let go

it doesn't care
about how I feel
or if I'm not well
and trying to heal

or maybe it does
and provides healing for free
sharing its secrets
for its life to see

I should have thanked it
for all of the above
its support and knowing
with healing and love

it always provides
    all that we need
an abundance of wellness
    that we eat and breathe

grounded in wisdom
    the land and the seas
in all of creation
    how could this be?

on top of that
    along comes me
thinking I'm right
    believing I'm free

Yes, right you are
    when in your right mind
and free to believe
    to love and to find

more of the same
    love's infinite supply
you had asked me how
    but the question is why

because that is me
    and so are you
and only as love
    we can be and do

that's what is real
and makes life renew
so I will tell you
in a verse or two

life is temporary
and passes away
and so does the sadness
but the love always stays

that is why
and what you will find
you are made for love
from the love of mine

Why again?

To know only love
is to know nothing less,
then you can express
only love at its best

you will always be
as you look you will see
you had asked me why
and said 'along comes me'

that's really it
*   and here's a suggestion*
you can be the answer
*   instead of the question*

there are only three words
*   you can ever be*
every question's answer is
*   'Love is me'*

that's what the world needs

SUFFERING

Is it possible to not suffer in life?
A healed mind means not suffering. Life-mind does not suffer in hope, love, and wonder.

What about forgiving ourselves and others?
All flows healing into the Light Mind, opening into the Light Mind of Godness.

Is it possible to heal the life-mind of all fear and regret, guilt and shame, etc.?
Healing means hoping, loving, and wondering in life while loving yourself in it.

What is a good reminder?
All of nature loving life, meaning allowing life to open into God Mind.

HEALING OUR LIFE-MINDS

What is the best way to heal our life-minds?

A wall in the life-mind allows only so much water over the dam. A healed life-mind has a lower wall of fear.

How can we lower the wall of fear?

Allow life-mind's fears less attention, allow filaments healing open into lightness and Godliness—hope, love, and charity.

To all of life including ourselves.

A hope has lighted love, love has lighted charity, and charity lights open Godliness— healing life-mind in the Light Mind of Godness.

Illuminated in meaning.

And healing open in life's hope, love, and charity. All opposing meanings are illusions.

It's Raining Somewhere

God doesn't know
  fear or pain
guilt or shame
    doubt or pain

and water can't know
    what a drought really is
and a lack of rain
    to rain can't exist

and what is lack
    but an absence of
whatever it is
    is God only love?

to allow or resist
    knowing God is this
to connect or miss
    love only gives

You know a lot
   of things that I'm not
but I wouldn't be proud
   and I have no doubt

that knowing and perceiving
   are two different things
perception requires judgment
   and the discernment it brings

to shape your thoughts
   feelings and beliefs
to avoid true healing
   or to be at peace

in your mind and heart
   from where you start
and to know the truth
   at least in part

that it's raining somewhere
   at any given time
love and abundance
   to your heart from mine

Secret of the Universe

**Please tell me a Secret of the Universe—
not that it will be a secret anymore.**
*Allow life more of life's adventures, and heal
in mostly allowing hope, love, and wonder
as life opens a healing portal in time.
All time heals in the life-minds allowing
hope, love, and wonder.
Allowing love means not allowing most
thoughts of non-loving kindness toward life,
and yourself healing in it.
Not allowing fear means not living half in
the past and half in the future.
An adventure motions in the moment,
allowing hope, love, and wonder.
Healing in time, life heals loving in each
moment.*

Life is an adventure.
A loving life, healing adventure in time.

Love is real, healing is real, and time is not.

All healing is in the life-mind. All love heals in the Light Mind of Godness, all healing in the illusion of momentary timelines.

So we heal either way, in time or in timelessness?

All healing in the Light Mind of Godness willingly.

The Light Mind of Godness doesn't really gain anything if our adventure in time is an illusion and we heal either way.

All healing in the Light Mind of Godness alternates in and out of life-minds, illuminating in the Mind of Godness, allowing God 'infinite loving in life.'

Living and dying are healing, and healing is real. Loving life allows God, loving life is healing. Is that right?

All a wonderful adventure the Mind of God lives, yes.

So it is God's adventure, allowing 'infinite loving in life'?

Alternating half in the life-mind, and half healing in the Light Mind of Godness.

Is God having a good adventure?

A hopeful, loving life moment of wonder,
yes.

How can readers have a wonder-ful life?

Become like little children—loving life in
hope, illuminating in wonder.

The world could use more love and hope,
and there is plenty to wonder about.

Hope lives in the mind, love lives in the
heart, and wonder lives in the space in
between.

Should each person try to heal negative
thoughts or memories by forgiving them,
thanking them, or loving them?

Allowing them life means loving them.
Allowing them healing means forgiving
them.
Allow them into the Light Mind of Godness
to heal.
Healing them in the Light Mind of Godness
releases them.

So when negative thoughts or memories
come up, I will forgive them and allow
them into the Light Mind of Godness to
heal.

All healing in an instant.

I hear a bird singing outside. They don't hold onto negative thoughts, do they?
All healing in each moment and in each loving song, no.

I will try to be like that.
All of life lives healing outside in nature, manifesting life in the Mind of God.

HOPE, LOVE, AND WONDER

To live in hope
   love and wonder
like little children
   8 and under

didn't they learn
   from where they came
that life has limits
   except fear and pain?

will they have to learn
   to hope in vain
to be afraid
   and to live in shame?

or will they retain
   these things that they know
their hope, love, and wonder
   as they play and they grow?

These are the tools
  when a child arrives
it needs to live
  to thrive and survive

a heart and a mind
  and the space in between
is where we will meet
  to create as a team

hope in the mind
  imagines it real
and love in the heart
  knows how it feels

to wonder in time
  with our forces combined
and create what you want
  with thoughts that are kind

to make your own life
  of abundance and peace
all fears and pains
  are healed and released

that is our deal
  and together we'll find
hope, love, and wonder
  in our Godness of Mind

GOD, WHERE DO I START

Hope is the faith
   held in my mind
trusting in God
   in life I will find

goodness and peace
   with thoughts that are kind
love is increased
   and brought into time

love is the place
   held in my heart
of knowing in life
   I am never apart

from all of creation
   that is made as One
and in my relation
   which never is done

wonder is the space
   where hope and love meet
a place of allowing
   creation to be

which makes me wonder
   about my part
as Oneness and forever
   God, where do I start

ONE AND ONE MAKES YOU

Begin by forgiving
yourself and others
since both are one
    you'll forgive one another

and by loving yourself
    which also includes them
but starts with you
    so now is when

you power creation
    from inside your heart
the eternal cycle
    that requires a spark

subatomic reactions
    lighting within
to create your world
    the universe begins

to rock your world
    projecting it new
the one thing that's real
    love directed from you

Why does it seem
   that hope disappears
if life is a dream
   and why are there fears?

Fear is a sign
   that your connection is low
and you're willing to believe
   what I'll never know

there is only love
   the energy of creation
flowing through you
   and your imagination

making your life
   and all that unfolds
out of my control
   or so I am told

your life is a dream
   and I have no doubt
that it seems very real
   but won't heal without

love flowing through
   what you see and do
a collaborative effort
   between me and you

to think we're apart
  in a world gone mad
with both light and dark
  good and bad

at least in your dream
  that you believe to be true
what you have conceived
  I've agreed to it too

some people say
  one and one makes two
but if I'm One and love
  then one and one makes you

Laws of the Universe

Are there Laws of the Universe?
Love in mind heals in action—meaning love motions only toward God. Nothing heals in darkness.

How many laws are there?
As many as life needs to know God—only one more. Hope, love, and wonder manifest healing in the life-mind, opening into the Light Mind of Godness.

You say, "Nothing heals in darkness." What is 'darkness'?
A life-mind opened allowing potential for hating life and anything in it, including life in the timeline chosen.

What happens if someone hates life, or a large part of life, or themselves?
Allowing hatred means not healing into the Light Mind of Godness.
Allowing hatred will manifest more to hate.

I guess I need to avoid what we call 'politics' at all cost.

Allow only loving peaceful thoughts.

You will help me, correct?

Always and at all times.

Thank you.

Love healing in time means only love is real.

I'll Love Being You

Is the purpose of life
to discern truth from illusion
the wheat from the chaff
    wisdom from confusion?

talk about endless
    and I'm not keeping score
but if lies had value
    we'd never be poor

What are lies
    and what are they for?
you can lie to yourself
    and nothing more

close your eyes
    and use me as your guide
the truth all lies
    inside at your core

so let me ask you
  if the lies are disguised
or can you see the love
  can you gladly try?

and if you do
  it's where I come through
you'll be what you see
  and I'll love being you

Hope

What should we always hope for?
Allowing love into the Light Mind, opening to God Mind.

By loving life?
All healing in timelines opened in progression, healed in an instant, illuminating in the Mind of God in eternity.

Does God Mind need us to have the challenges and failings in a world of duality, so we can forgive and heal, only to illuminate and perpetuate God in eternity?
A healed mind illuminates in eternity, opening more life-mind lifetimes to love and heal in—so life means healing, allowing, and loving in time, or not. Life means healing and motioning toward love, or God Mind.

But does God Mind need it?

All hope in the life-mind will heal open the Light Mind into God Mind—so no, healing in life motions toward God Mind, healing in time or timelessness—meaning God Mind allows the illusion of life in time. Allowing will replace needing in the life-mind also.

No News

(FROM ONE POSSIBLE FUTURE)

I don't need news
  the corporate views
just tell me something
    new I can use

did they finally bomb
    every country on earth
it was probably deserved
    women and children first

did the government go broke
    having squandered our wealth
on wars and reports
    of financial health

I thought that their role
    was to keep the peace
so we could grow old
    and live as we please

what if it closed
   and they all went home
to do something useful
   leave everyone alone

to keep what we earn
   and people would learn
as self-sufficient
   communities return

united in ideals
   of honor and trust
for the common good
   and the good is just

freedom to express
   to be and create
with grievances addressed
   in a healthy debate

the only tax
   is some of our time
do unto others
   is the law that binds

cooperative living
   of learning and giving
where competing just means
   how fast we're forgiving

the news today
    was the meal we made
and we had discussed
    what we could trade

if anyone's alive
    and if others survived
we've had no news
    since the bombs arrived

To Know You Are Me

I can't explain
your need for pain
it's what you would call
   totally insane

more wealth or power
   and control at all costs
or in religious beliefs
   where the meaning is lost

being God
   is knowing full well
that you will create
   your heaven or hell

you will also heal
   either way
in life or in death
   so I'm going to say

that it's up to you
   but you also forgot
that you are gods too
   believing you're not

you can create more
    destruction and war
or believe in yourselves
    and what gods are for

to heal in life
    and to heal each other
to feel what's right
    and to love one another

there's a lot to love
    and nothing to hate
and inside your heart
    is heaven's gate

to loving yourself
    where love will create
in our hearts as One
    where I can relate

if all that you think
    and all that you see
allows love and peace
    then we can agree

there's only one thing
    it's how heaven will be
knowing God is love
    is to know you are me

Most Important Thing in Life

What is the most important thing in life?
Allowing life-mind light healing into the Light Mind of Godness.

By reducing our fears?
And loving life in each moment.

What if moments are stressful or fearful?
Allow love lightness to lessen them, healing them into the Light Mind illumination of Oneness.
The life-mind heals open into Light Mind, allowing healing into Oneness. Allowing means filaments healing open illuminated in life-mind.

Will an affirmation help us to do that?
Affirm Light Mind in the life-mind by acknowledging Oneness in everything.

What about twoness and separation?
A healed life-mind loves Oneness allowing illusions of twoness.

I need to practice that.

A filament heals open each time, allowing healing into the Light Mind of Godness.

So we really just need to see Oneness in a world of twoness and duality—twoness as our perception of being apart from God, and duality as our perception of opposites—light/dark, good/bad, etc.

All and each meet in the neutral center, allowing healing into the Light Mind of Godness.

Please explain.

All Oneness healing in a perception of twoness in life—willingly operating in windows of place and time opening in the life-mind—will motion or not, meaning toward Oneness or not.

So Oneness does not need healing, just our perception of twoness has a need for healing which is achieved by motioning toward Oneness?

A life-mind has only one purpose—allowing Oneness, timelessness, and lightness into life-mind, healing open into Oneness.

How do we do that?

Will Oneness not allow healing, and not allow life-mind motion illuminated in time? Healing life-mind means opening into the Light Mind of Godness, illuminating in Oneness. Oneness illuminates life-mind only in love.

Which we allow or not allow.

Allow means only one thing—one life-mind willfully opening to the Light Mind of Godness.

Should we focus on allowing only thoughts of love and Oneness?

Light means open in a window of time, allowing love to heal a life-mind in lightness—or non-love to punish a life-mind in needing lightness.

How do we allow more lightness?

A life-mind heals in open portals illuminated in windows of time, illuminating life-mind healing open into Oneness.

Open portals of light remain open by loving yourself in them. Love opens them, and loving life will keep them open.

I AM ME

Fear of losing
  fear of winning
the root of all evil
    has fear at the beginning

and losing what?
    money and status
prestige and appearance
    esteem apparatus

or to lose it all
    life and limb
does it count as a loss
    if I'm afraid to win?

and winning what?
    what is to gain?
just more protection
    to avoid any pain

I can also learn
    why we came
to grow in awareness
    to know and to change

and change to what?
   why and what for?
Infinite and fearless
   when less is more

to be only love
   or to eternally try
until we are One
   and that is why

That all sounds fine
   I appreciate the reply
but if we are One
   then who am I?

You are my savior
   and you help me to see
that if I could change
   you are how I would be

always loving
   and only love I would see
being One with you
   I AM glad I AM me

My Moment With You

What will be here
in a thousand years
will the sun still shine
to dry all the tears?

will there still be rain
to wash away the pain?
will the earth remain
with nothing to gain?

will the seasons renew
the way that they do
except for the fears
left by me and you?

how would it be
with no imbalance or strife
could the earth go on
without us in life?

maybe so, well
definitely yes
the life that is gone
will be us I guess

why can't we
   just live in peace
and appreciate life
   to let love increase?

You said the key words
   'love and peace'
'renew and you'
   those are the keys

to survive and thrive
   and I'll tell you why
to know the joy
   of being alive

and it doesn't matter
   where or when
you will grow in awareness
   now or then

Are you trying to say
   that the life we know
will be gone one day
   with nothing to show?

Every day ends
   to start over anew
except for one thing
   love coming from you

that lives forever
   in my eternal mind
the love I could never
   hope to find

so I chose you
   to create what I could
my co-creator
   of love and good

but you should know
   in my infinite view
there's no thousand years
   just my moment with you

[or should I say
   'as you' or 'for you'
there's no time at all
   after or before you]

The Biggest Mystery in Life

What is the biggest mystery in life?
*All life heals in love in time. Love means
healing instantly.*

Because there is no time?
*Allowing love time allows life lower or
higher manifestations of loving oneself
willingly or not—mindlessly, or mind purely
healing in the Light Mind of Godness.*

How can we do that?
*Allow love, life, and the Light Mind of
Godness only one thing—love healing in
each moment willingly.*

Please explain.
*Allow life's manifestations of lower mental
activity a lifetime to heal, instantly healing
them in life willingly by loving yourself.
Loving yourself means loving all of life in all
of its manifestations. Light Mind of Godness
heals life instantly, allowing the life
manifestation healing in the lightness of
being, illuminating healed, flowing in life.*

ALL OF ALL THAT IS

That one is giving
    only to himself
and that one is living
    in her personal hell

this one is judging
    what I can do well
the ego's opinion
    'I' can always tell

but the ego knows nothing
    except its pain from disdain
its every derision
    is division in vain

what does it gain
    to be always right
totally insane
    to keep up the fight

It misinterprets
the meaning of 'One'
yours or mine
and it thinks it won

talk about separate
and I can't judge it as wrong
but being One in spirit
was the One all along

until the ego thought
I am separate from that
and ever since
has tried to get back

not finding peace
just needs to attack
learning the hard way
believing in lack

you can turn it down
and undo its control
by giving my spirit
the leading role

which brings you closer
to Oneness with me
from denial to acceptance
of the way to see

I am love and light
   who's to say 'I am right'
to be free is to be
   One in spiritual sight

you will know inside
   that I am always here
the body will die
   and there's nothing to fear

again in my Oneness
   with only truth to hear
love and peacefulness
   and what I hold dear

is for you to realize
   eternal bliss
and the joy of expressing
   all of All that Is

Source Energy

What is the source of Source energy or God energy?

All of life's love illumination winding around the right brain, healing the left brain—originates in Light Minds of Godness illuminated in loving life, holding the window of hope, love, and wonder open—allowing more illuminations healing the left brain, or life-mind.

What is the source of the light?

All healing in the life-mind creates more light, illuminating life. Hope, love, and wonder open the light window or portal in each life-mind.

And the healing is what creates the light?

A healing will keep lighting in timelessness, or eternity.

Very cool.

All of healing in timelines means healing into eternity.

And I am an eternal being healing in timelines?

Yes, one life-mind in one lifetime healing into one God Mind. Nothing heals in darkness.

Hey, we have access to a lot of darkness here.

All will heal in timelines of life, making more light.

Can we actively heal darkness?

Allow only light into your mind, and only light will manifest healing wherever it shines.

Very cool again.

All healing into the Light Mind of Godness.

Which comes first, the healing or the light?

All will manifest at once, meaning there is no 'before.'

Was this healing moment of illusion your idea?

Loving life is my idea, healing in life is your idea.

So that I could experience your idea?

*As willingly loving life and yourself in it,
yes.*

Then what?

*A Light Mind opens into God Mind allowing
more light into life-mind, healing into Light
Mind, and so on.*

ONLY ONE YOU

What is the meaning
   behind my purpose
and why am I dreaming
   this three-ring circus?

*To see what you are
   and what you are being
first see what you're not
   and where love is agreeing*

*then you will feel
   the whole expanding
right into you
   for your soul understanding*

Why would I want
   to see what I'm not
then see all as One
   I knew, but forgot

I am the love
  and so are you
but only as One
  although it seems like two

healing flawed beliefs
  opposing energies release
creating more light
  to infinitely increase

making your world
  with the truth that you use
the cosmos is designed
  for you to choose

from multiple views
  as you decide
what's true inside
  where I am your guide

being only One
  and all that One includes
life has two sides
  for only One you

(illusion is side two)

Now They Are Light

I confess
　　I was not at my best
the dozens of times
　　when I failed the test

and went out of my lane
　　out of my league
no one to blame
　　only me

maybe the poem
　　should end right here
along with the shame
　　the same every year

What you can do
　　to be truly healed
is to take your regrets
　　how you truly feel

roll them up tight
  shrink-wrapped and sealed
hold them in the light
  no need to kneel

You can have them
  just let me know
I've added a label
  they are ready to go

I will recycle
  transmute and shift
repurpose and repackage
  what you have shipped

they were kind of heavy
  but that's alright
I have healed them with love
  now they are light

Why Do We Incarnate?

Why do we incarnate into human form?
*Housing one life-mind in one life body
allows hoping, loving, and wondering—
willingly opening into windows of time and
placement.*

Do humans live more than once?
*Life heals open many windows in timelines
as life-mind alternating in life-mind and
God Mind allowing purity in hope, love, and
wonder.*

**Are the windows in timelines all opened
simultaneously?**
*Allowing one to willingly purify, heal, and
close in a progression of love—all healing in
an outward and inward spiral—illuminates
all of them in a life-mind spiral on the ladder
of allowing healing in a life-mind moment,
in each of life-mind's timelines opening into
the Light Mind of Godness.*

I will try not to get drawn into any more fear or negativity. Will that advance my lifetimes up the spiral?

All heal in unison in hope, love, and wonder—alternating onto the next higher plane on the ladder.

Does 'hope' mean holding a vision of positive outcomes, and 'love' mean loving life and yourself in it, and 'wonder' mean allowing the miracles to manifest in your life?

Alternatively illuminating in the life-mind, and healing in the Light Mind of Godness, yes—alternating on each long leg of the spiral.

Do you mean like a DNA spiral?

All DNA spirals in a long line illuminating in time and placement.

Where does the light or biophotons in our DNA come from?

All light coming out of DNA, alternating in the life-mind and the Light Mind of Godness modulates high or low depending on the life-mind's willingness to allow hope, love, and wonder to gain light or to lose light.

Does the light transfer information both ways like an optical router?

Allowing light only transfers information to you. All light moves in the outward direction.

Does the light originate at the Mind of God?

As the Light Mind of Godness, yes.

Can we send light or information to God that way?

A life-mind in illumination of total enlightening links to the Mind of God—hope, love, and wonder in total awe of the Mind of God.

A Few Kind Words

I'm running out
   of time on earth
  where I came to find
  a few kind words

it started out right
   or that's what I heard
then I had to fight
   for what I deserved

but fight implies conflict
   and a need to win
and the light of my sight
   should have been from within

like peace and love
   happiness and health
all kind words must first
   come from myself

Where Does

Consciousness Originate?

Where does consciousness originate?
Alternating half illuminated in life-mind,
and half in the Light Mind of Godness as one
light glowing. Half healing in time, and half
healed in timelessness—life glows
light allowing love, allowing life, allowing
healing, allowing love, and so on. Healing
allows filaments to illuminate, lighting open
portal universes of reality—not lighting or
lighting healing in time and place.

So there is a constant exchange of
information or light between life-mind
and the Light Mind of Godness?
Allowing life-mind healing in time.
All of life-mind illuminates in the Light Mind
of Godness, and loses light in the life-mind.
A healing illumination in the life-mind
allows infinite love and light into life's portal
realities.

Is 'infinite love and light' the Light Mind of
Godness?

All lightness and all lovingness—all motion
life, meaning all atoms are love light
machines, holistically healing life.

How can we alternate more into the Light Mind of Godness?

Illuminate life in all timelessness knowing
healing in all timelines by purifying
thoughts, only hearing loving peaceful
thoughts.

Negative thoughts come up to be healed, forgiven, purified—which then allows more infinite love and light into a person's life?

Love is a potion, healing emotions
loving my life, is my one devotion
lighting my life, healing my fear
love in my mind, in stillness I hear

That's a great affirmation—a mantra which would change a person's life?

Yes, highly loving life makes more life to love.

Making a feedback loop that increases exponentially like a spiral?

All healing in life moves in a spiral
motion, willingly or not—meaning in light
or non-light, higher or lower, gaining light
or losing light in the DNA of life.

I'm Not Keeping Score

There's not much in it
   for me anymore
      just more disappointments
   and I'm not keeping score

*Yes, you are
   and you're totally sure
that all of your hopes
   are worth hoping for*

*you had hoped for peace
   and the love which you feel
both timeless and real
   to be eternally healed*

*you can hope and love
   and look for wonder too
but where that lives
   is inside of you*

*that's my secret
   and all you will need
if you work with these
   you will be working with me*

creating from your core
to open new doors
I'm not keeping score
but we'll keep making more

from love and peace
they will increase
surrounding your dreams
as they heal into me

which makes more light
opening windows in time
every thought and choice
will start to align

your heart and mind
how life was designed
always in motion
for you to find

and light your way back
not an easy climb
where thoughts can attack
and hide my shine

allow them to go
and love their release
then you will know
how to make peace

Yeah, well
　　I guess you could say
if it's not loving or healed
　　then it would be fake

It's fake in a sense
　　that it only exists
to be forgiven and healed
　　or it will persist

to only make more
　　not what you wished
disappointments galore
　　and only more of this

feel your love shine
　　peace in all directions
and bless the divine
　　in its wonderful perfection

by loving what is
　　you're the healing ointment
there is no 'dis'
　　in life's appointment

scheduled in time
　　you're doing just fine
as the healer assigned
　　to light the worlds of mine

ONLY AS WE

I'm still disappointed
  and feel disjointed
like I was appointed
  as a fly in the ointment

talking to Oneness
  is all very good
but out here in the field
  it's less understood

that we choose with our minds
  and create with our hearts
through all lines in time
  that are opened in part

for us to heal
  so God is revealed
and together we feel
  only love can be real

when unconcealed
  that was our deal
right from the source
  which is us, of course

I'd like to suggest
  just as a test
and even insist
  for you to do this

try being two
  and what would you do
if you were like me
  and not the One you?

You just answered
  your very own question
and I've taken you up
  on your suggestion

we are always one
  believing we're two
but as one of each
  unique in each view

now I'd like to suggest
  just as a test
and even insist
  for you to do this

imagine you're me
  and what you would do
as my twoness to see
  how Oneness could be

Well, I don't know
  if I agree with you
when I look around
  and see more than two

and I'm quite disturbed
  to tell you the truth
you've probably heard
  and I can give you proof

that life is a mass
  of contradictions
and in time will pass
  with my convictions

*Again you answered
  your very own question
all will pass
  and you'll retain the lesson*

*that there is only love
  and only one me
and only as you
  we can only be*

only as we

MAGICAL FEEDBACK LOOP

Is the universe a magical feedback loop that reinforces only how I feel about myself?

A love loop winding through glowing openings in life-minds, healing into the Light Mind of Godness, opening into the Mind of God.

Are 'glowing openings' portals in the life-mind that are lighted open by peaceful, loving thoughts?

Yes, opened in time and placement in all timelines in eternity—all healing in the Light Mind of Godness, and opening into the Mind of God. Life-mind lights open Light Mind, allowing opening of God Mind.

It sounds like the 'love loop' is the most important thing for us to maintain.

A life-mind lighting into Light Mind, allowing God Mind in life will manifest more light in life, meaning more life-mind healing—illuminating in hope, love, and wonder.

A negative feedback loop by definition becomes progressively worse, so a positive feedback loop becomes progressively better?

Healing in the life-mind will only manifest more healing illuminations in Light Mind— allowing more light, as a lighted candle illuminates a large room. Healing in life-mind heals in all timelines, allowing Light Mind instant opening into God Mind.

Any negative thought or activity closes portals in the life-mind, which I understand are like flowers that open into the light?

A life-mind portal manifesting healing in illumination must be opened in hope, love, and wonder.

Do I hope, love, and wonder enough?

I hope, love, and wonder about it.

ITS OWN REWARD

L et this sink in
 that there is no reward
in the outer world
   unless moving toward

peace and oneness
   our being the same
to advance and heal
   it's why we came

to face our challenges
   designed to reveal
inner courage and love
   by how we feel

on an obstacle course
   that seems very real
there's no going back
   and no force can unseal

what the soul records
   internally stored
our eternal award
   is its own reward

C+

Y ou would think
I'm not afraid to fail
I've had enough practice
left a steady trail

of poor judgment
missteps and errors
regrettable mistakes
now memorable terrors

Think of life
as learning classes
where grades are for improvement
and your effort passes

much more than that
your score would reach
to the higher range
so you could teach

that the lesson is
　　the lesson you earn
from each experience
　　you had to learn

a better thought
　　to know and discern
what can't be taught
　　so each gets their turn

to learn from mistakes
　　and repeat them no more
to take a life course
　　and get a good score

you are given chances
　　to retake each test
move on to the next
　　and forgive the rest

that is the way
　　to be a success
and in the end you can say
　　I did my best

(you will also be judged
　　on the effort you made
but will be grading yourself
　　on Graduation Day)

[I see you just gave
    yourself a grade
the course isn't over
    there's still time for an 'A'

and I'll give you hints
    tell you what to say
love is the answer
    the rest of the way]

CONCENTRIC CIRCLES

The morning that Malaysia Air flight 370 disappeared in 2014, you had said that "it flew into the nearest line of time and space inside the earth's grid and keeps on flying..." What is that?

A low line, a middle line, and a high line in the life-mind's portal of reality—meaning life-mind's open portal of time and place, not lighting or lighting into the Light Mind of Godness—alternating in time and no time, or timelessness—astounding in lighting life open in pure worlds of life loving life—are held together with large links of life-mind love/non-love pulsing winds of neutrality.

Do the low line, middle line, and high line circle the earth?

All in concentric circles, yes.

One of each, or in a grid of each?

A long line of each, a line always sweeping along a light/non-light, love/non-love new day opening in time.

So the lines pass over us at sunrise and sunset?

All in a line, meaning a circle—and not moving, yes.

How high up is the low line?

About 8 miles in the upper atmosphere.

And the middle line?

About 34 miles in the stratosphere.

How high is the high line?

About 144 miles in the ionosphere.

Fibonacci proportions noted.

All of healing in life-mind is in proportion to loving life and loving itself in life, willingly allowing light in each morning—lighting in the Light Mind's portals in the light body— lighting a new day to live, love, and heal.

The concentric circles around the earth— the high line, the middle line, and the low line—is mass consciousness in them?

Allowing maligned or aligned healing manifestations illuminating in time slowly, yes.

Please explain.

A healing, peaceful wish illuminates, opening portals in the lower circle, largely manifesting in time. Healing in time means hoping life manifests open lower portals illuminated healed into reality. Healing in reality means lighting hope in the mind. Hope highlights the life-mind vectors that light open portals in the lower circle, manifesting them in time.

Are peaceful thoughts vectors?

All loving, peaceful, and grateful thoughts are life-mind vectors that light open the manifesting portals aligning healing light, allowing the manifestation. Nothing heals in darkness.

Portals are in the lower circle and opened by peaceful, loving thoughts?

Aligning, illuminating, and manifesting in time, yes.

What is the middle circle?

All higher illuminated beings of love, willingly moving into timelines life-minds create, hoping to heal. Love heals, highlighting the middle circle, allowing healing manifestations in the lower circle.

Aligning the life-mind and the Light Mind means hoping, loving, healing, and gratefully wondering—owning life half in each circle.

Is the lower circle the life-mind, and the middle circle the Light Mind?

Alternating healing in time and placement, yes.

What is the upper circle?

The Light Mind of Godness, meaning only pure love and lightness of being.

Is it the energy of God?

All loving, healing, grateful, wonderful life-mind hope illuminates in the lower circle in time, to open portals in the middle circle—all illuminating healed in the upper circle, manifesting into reality.

Fibonacci number noun

🔖 Save Word

Fi·bo·nac·ci number | \ ˌfē-bə-ˈnä-chē- 🔊, ˌfi-bə- \

a never-ending sequence starting with 0 and 1, and continuing by adding the previous two numbers together. Fibonacci numbers are called the "golden ratio" because of their frequency in the natural world.

CROSSING THE LINE

How many times
 will I cross the line
2x per day
    that we are assigned

light shines and defines
    the past now behind
from darkness to light
    3 rings are aligned

with each new day
    for us to know
as above
    so it is below

lighting the mind
    from high to low
in loving yourself
    your life will show

that love is the meaning
    life loves to give
from dawn to dusk
    it loves you to live

THE MIND OF GOD

I don't really meditate, but would it be most useful to clear my mind at sunrise and make peaceful, loving wishes while the 3 concentric circles are overhead?

Yes, loving, hoping, and wondering illuminates them.

Are deceased souls or spirits in the lower circle?

All of them are healed into the outer circle, or Light Mind of Godness.

What is the astral plane?

A flowing portal, meaning the space between the circles.

Where are malicious or unhealed spirits?

Lower in the lower circle of life-mind.

Are our spirit guides in the middle circle?

Almost all are in the middle circle, some are in the lower, and some are in the outer.

Are angels in the outer circle?

Allowing love half in the Light Mind, as One in the Mind of God, yes.

Does the outer circle extend outward infinitely?

The Mind of God could not extend outward in timelessness without your life-mind extending it inward in time.

Why not?

Portals life-mind opens allow Mind of God or not.

Blocking God?

Life-mind allows or not allows. The Mind of God loves always and infinitely, glowing open portals in the life-mind in all of its lifetimes, healed in the Light Mind, and opening into the Mind of God.

Where is God?

Always and everywhere life-mind loves— healing the life-mind, opening the Light Mind—willingly allowing Mind of God a life-mind hoping, loving, and manifesting wonders in time.

an·gel

/ˈānjəl/

See definitions in:

(All) (Religion) (Numismatics) (Aviation · *Informal*)

noun
plural noun: **angels**

a spiritual being believed to act
as an attendant, agent,
or messenger of God

THE HIGHER PLANES

Is fear only in the earth plane?

All willingly closing portals to the higher planes.

Is the lower circle life-mind, the middle circle Light Mind, and the outer circle the Mind of God?

All in concentric rings around the earth, yes.

Do the rings have names?

All of the lower energies are life-mind, higher energies are Light Mind, and the highest energy of love is God Mind.

How do we align with the higher energies?

Allow only loving, peaceful thoughts— hoping, loving, and wondering aligns the lower, middle, and outer rings in each life-mind's timelines.

In that alignment a person can manifest what they want, but at that point they probably don't want for anything.

Allowing replaces wanting.

By allowing only love, it allows safety and prosperity, etc.?

Allowing in the life-mind heals in the Light Mind, and lights into the Mind of God.

If I allow only peaceful loving thoughts, then my mind heals higher up into the middle circle or Light Mind, and then lights into the Mind of God?

Loving life means healing into the Light Mind, opening healed into the Mind of God.

Peaceful loving thoughts can also be wishes, which heal in the Light Mind, and will then manifest into reality?

Allowed to heal into reality, yes.

Allowed by the life-mind holding it only as a peaceful loving wish?

Allowing life healing manifestations to create in time, yes.

Love creates life to allow love, and so on.

Willingly or not, yes.

Allowed by our minds or not.

Healing or not.

You Have the Time

Fabulous errors
   and brilliant mistakes
even the worst ones
   were still pretty great

I have to love them
   see them in reverse
some of the best ones
   could have been worse

*That is right
   they're done and healed
creating more light
   for life to reveal*

*that it heals itself
   and lives in time
creating more life
   that lights in my mind*

lighting up yours
  where you can choose
to allow it in
  or find an excuse

to block it out
  and hide my shine
but that's okay
  I have time

(or should I say
  that you will find
I am timeless
  and you have the time)

THE PLANES OF LIGHTNESS

When people die, it is reported that they experience going into or through a tunnel to a lighted expansive space at the end of the tunnel. What is the tunnel?

A long life-mind portal connection to the Light Mind middle circle of healing.

34 miles above the earth?

Flowing and healing into the Mind of God which starts 144 miles above the earth.

Well, there you go—I mean, there you are...there I go.

Allowing Mind of God in life means not going anywhere to heal.

Since the concentric circles around the earth are always at the dividing line of night and day, is that part of the reason we live in a world of duality—light/dark, good/bad, love/fear?

Allowing both love and feeling the illusion of fear in the life-mind portal opening, yes.

Portals are in our DNA, and open or close depending on our thoughts and intentions?

Illuminating in love, or darkening in non-love.

What do the portals connect or open to?

An illuminated portal opens healing in the Light Mind of Godness—alternating in the life-mind.

How does it connect to the middle and lower circles if it is in our DNA?

Alternating in the light/non-light Flow-er of Life in each life-mind's heart, aligning or maligning the life-mind's manifestations.

There is no time or space in the circles since they are stationary?

All timelines are in the Light Mind middle circle. All healing in the Light Mind manifests in reality in time, opening into the life-mind's timeline in perfect time—allowing the manifestation to live in one timeline.

Do the circles have a width?

A half inch approximately.

Why so thin?

A film only needs a layer of light/non-light to project hope, love, and wonder to the Light Mind.

Projecting outward?

Not outward, higher in the planes of lightness.

So We'll Eternally Be

L ast night I dreamt
 that I was forgiven
 and now I'm exempt
 from my attempts at living

I must be healed
 the guilt let me go
and the dream had revealed
 what I already know

that we each have one
 perfect diamond center
brilliant colors that shine
 when light's allowed to enter

Now or later
 that is your choice
and whichever is greater
 yours or my voice

moving forward
 a progression in time
and what time is for
 is to align with my mind

a glowing enhancement
  designed in the rings
another soul advancement
  is like having two wings

I'm on the right
  and you're on the left
we'll fly in the light
  and in the dark we will rest

every morning we'll sing
  the truth as it's said
and each new day will bring
  three rings overhead

so darkness disappears
  and in the light you can see
gone are your fears
  and you are infinitely me

love takes flight
  you are internally free
your healing makes light
  so we'll eternally be

Universal Intelligence

If I made a diagram of a person, the left brain hemisphere or life-mind connects to the lower circle around the earth?
Alternating open to the middle circle, or Light Mind as the left brain and right brain hemispheres align in loving life—healing into God Mind, or the outer circle.

Would the diagram show the right brain hemisphere connected to the middle circle around the earth?
Alternating healing and not healing, allowing or not allowing peaceful, loving thoughts.

Are the 3 concentric rings around the earth tuned to our left brain, right brain, and heart?
All in the Mind of God, yes.

Is 'tuned' the right word?
All healing in 'alignment' in the higher circles.

By having only peaceful loving thoughts?

Hoping, loving, and wondering in time, yes.

As they heal, they create light—which is the healed Light Mind of Godness that opens portals into the outer circle or God Mind?

All willingly healed in eternity.

Would my diagram show the person's heart connected to the outer circle?

Alternating in the middle and outer circles— allowing and healing, or not allowing and not healing.

Allowing peace and love?

Allowing peaceful, loving thoughts and actions—allow them to align in loving life. Life means healing into alignment.

God Mind is not limited to the outer circle, is it?

All healing into God Mind willingly heals open glowing portal universes, highlighting love and peace in the Mind of God.

Does our healing create universes?

A healed life-mind perpetuates all timelessness infinitely, allowing universes hope, love, and wonder.

In my diagram, does a peaceful, loving wish or thought connect vectors from the left brain, right brain, and heart–to the 3 concentric rings around the earth—all in alignment with each other, such as all in a 12 o'clock position?

A healed mind likens to that, yes.

Aligned in heart and mind?

Aligned in hope, love, and wonder.

And aligns with our soul?

Aligns hope in the mind with love in the heart, healing open into the Mind of God–lighting open universes in the Mind of God.

Infinitely?

All healing infinitely.

Does life mean healing now?

A world moves toward multiple universes in each moment–so life willingly heals them or not heals them now. Healing will light open new universes in the Mind of God.

Are we constantly splitting between two worlds, healed and needing to be healed?

All healing in the mind or in time, yes.

To eventually be healed?

All healing in the Mind of God, yes.

Am I healing?

And Light Mind of Godness illuminates.

Creating a new universe?

A healing illuminating the Light Mind of Godness always opens new universal intelligence in the Mind of God as universes, purely as the means to Oneness healing twoness in hope, love, and wonder—all healing in the Mind of God.

Do I create a new universe for myself with each choice, thought, or action?

Yes—one, then another, and so on.

AFTERWORD

It is interesting to note that in *Journey of Souls* by Michael Newton, Ph.D., he states that "for thousands of years, the people of Mesopotamia believed the gates into and out of heaven lay at opposite ends of the great curve of the Milky Way, called the River of Souls."

In his hypnotherapy practice, he discovered that subjects in deep trance could report to him accounts of leaving their bodies after death, and about life in the spirit world between lifetimes. They describe going away from the earth in a tunnel, and in the chapter "The Advanced Soul," he writes that subjects describe "traveling as souls on lines which curve, and seem round to them... Some have called this place the heart, or breath of God."

GLOSSARY

ONENESS: Infinity healed illuminating in God Mind.

GOD MIND: All twoness healed and illuminating in Oneness.

LIFE-MIND: Left-brain hemispheres healing and illuminating in an open portal in time.

LIGHT MIND: Right-brain hemispheres opening into the Mind of God.

LIGHT MIND OF GODNESS: Alternating healing and healed in life-mind allowing God Mind.

PORTAL: An opening in DNA, lighting open in God Mind.

FILAMENTS: Undulating light sensors, halting or allowing light into life through life's DNA.

LIGHT: Life-minds healing half in timelines, and half in timelessness.

TIMELESSNESS: All healed in God Mind, not in life-mind.

TIME: The lightness of being alternating in the life-mind as the illusion of moving in a progression.

NATURE: All of life healing in the Mind of God.

DEATH: Lighting open healed infinitely in Oneness.

INFINITY: All one instant in the Mind of God.

About the Author

Paul Gorman is an architect and poet
living in Maryland, USA.

*"The scientist has marched in
and taken the place of the poet.
But one day somebody will find
the solution to the problems of the world
and remember, it will be a poet,
not a scientist."*
                    —Frank Lloyd Wright

email contact: gormanpoetry@gmail.com

Made in the USA
Columbia, SC
21 September 2022